THE **POWER** OF **CASH** DEALS

Never Underestimate the

POWER

OF

CASH

DEALS

By Edward E. Sanders

Certified Purchasing Manager

BLUE CHIP Publishing

Written by Edward E. Sanders

Certified Purchasing Manager

Edited by Joe VanderZanden

Illustrations by Larry Sidebottom

Book design by Blake McKinney

Cover design by Richard Jester

Library of Congress Catalog Card Number: 93-70514

ISBN 0-9635724-0-7

Blue Chip Publishing

661 High Street NE
Salem, OR 97301-2439

Dedicated to the memory of my dad,
Louis Sanders,
who at an early age taught me the value of a hard earned dollar.

THE **POWER** OF **CASH** DEALS

Perspective

How to buy in the '90s

How should you be doing your buying in the '90s? The answer is simple, with skill and CASH; specifically, by using the skills of a professional buyer. Once you understand these skills, you should be able to effectively use them in every buying situation, coupled with the power of CASH.

However, the reality for most people is that cash is not a way of life or a plentiful commodity. So, to be able to take full advantage of the techniques that are presented in this book, you must be committed to developing a self discipline about personal money management and getting the most possible from intelligent buying.

This book explains professional buying skills and techniques that you will be able to immediately implement into your everyday buying behavior. The results should be revealed with some definite CASH savings to you.

Edward E. Sanders
Certified Purchasing Manager

Introduction

Before you begin to read this book

A. Know your buying-self well. Recognize your strengths and improve upon your weaknesses. Only then, can you become very skilled at buying and stretching your hard earned dollars. ANSWER the questions in Chapter One which will identify your current buying behavior.

B. Recognize that the '90s represent what can be the best of times or the worst of times for personal financial circumstances. So, take immediate steps to control your buying thirst, work hard at reducing your personal debt, and establish a program that can generate the cash that you would like to have for CASH DEALING.

C. Realize that the skills of cash buying can be learned by anyone who has the desire to possess them. Unlimited savings and returns can be the honest results of cash buying. Cash buyers in the '90s will definitely have strong deal making power, as is currently being reflected in an economy where cash is quickly becoming king.

Contents

Contents

A Look at Your Buying Self

Before the skills of cash buying can be recognized and acquired, you must first begin by identifying your present buying behavior. The **who, what, when, where, why, and how** of your current buying style should be intelligently analyzed. Quite simply, it is important to really know your buying self.

Answer the following questions by placing a check mark in the appropriate boxes.

NOTE: There are no correct or incorrect answers, or right or wrong methods, functions or procedures; the objective is to reflect a buying self that may or may not please you. Be honest with your answers and quickly check the things that come to mind first.

Who are you buying from right now?

That is, who do you personally deal with when buying products or services?
- ❐ store clerks
- ❐ friends in business
- ❐ relatives in business
- ❐ door-to-door salespeople
- ❐ catalog salespeople
- ❐ store owners or managers

Are you satisfied with the people you deal with when buying?
- ❐ yes
- ❐ no
- ❐ some of them
- ❐ some of them some of the time

Can you say "no" to these people when you sense that the price, service, or quality may not be fair?
- ❐ yes
- ❐ no
- ❐ some of them
- ❐ some of them some of the time

Do you believe that you are always getting the most competitive (lowest) prices from these people?
- ❐ yes, most of the time
- ❐ no, not always
- ❐ honestly don't know

Do you think that these people know their products/services well enough to honestly recommend the things that will best meet your needs; not necessarily the most expensive, the cheapest, or the things that they make the most profit from selling?
- ❐ yes, most of the time
- ❐ no, not always
- ❐ honestly don't know

What products and services are you currently buying?

- ❐ rent/house payment
- ❐ utilities: gas, electric, telephone
- ❐ auto: purchase payment or lease payment, maintenance
- ❐ insurances: auto, home, life, etc.
- ❐ home services: newspaper, cable TV, etc.
- ❐ food: grocery store, restaurants
- ❐ medical/dental
- ❐ health care: drug store products
- ❐ clothing and shoes
- ❐ banking services
- ❐ education: school tuition, books, etc.
- ❐ furniture
- ❐ appliances: kitchen, laundry, TV, compact disc player, etc.
- ❐ vacation travel
- ❐ entertainment gifts
- ❐ other _____

Are you satisfied with these purchases?
- ❐ yes, most of them
- ❐ no, none of them
- ❐ only some of them

List the items (if any) that are not satisfactory and you would not buy if you had the decision to make again: _____
_____
_____
_____
_____
_____

If you had to drastically reduce your spending, what things could you reasonably cut? (list)_____
_____
_____
_____
_____
_____

When do you buy?

For many people, a little of each.
- ❐ mornings
- ❐ afternoons
- ❐ evenings
- ❐ weekdays
- ❐ weekends
- ❐ end of the month
- ❐ slow business times
- ❐ busy times
- ❐ before holiday seasons

❒ during holiday seasons
❒ after holiday seasons
❒ during sales and promotions
❒ before fashion seasons begin
   (fall, winter, spring, summer)
❒ during fashion seasons
❒ after fashion seasons
   (bathing suits and straw hats in September)

Are you satisfied that you are getting the lowest possible prices at the times when you are buying?
❒ yes, most often
❒ no, not as often as I would like
❒ sometimes
❒ don't know, haven't thought about it

Do you think that some businesses continually promote sales and sale pricing to stimulate consumer buying?
❒ yes
❒ no
❒ don't know

What is your reaction to promotional advertising that is specifically directed toward price motivation; such as factory rebates, low financing rates, two-for-one coupons, half payments for a year, no payments for a year, this weekend only, etc?
❒ I often buy during these promotions and obtain good values
❒ I occasionally buy, but only the things that I really need and can afford
❒ I always shop the sales, for I can never pass up a good deal

When businesses continually offer merchandise at sale prices, how do you think they can afford to stay in business when they are always selling at those discounted prices?
- ❐ They know what they are doing and make up the difference by selling in volume quantities
- ❐ The original price of the merchandise was artificially marked-up, and in reality the sale price is probably the normal price that should be charged
- ❐ I have no idea, never thought about it

Where do you buy?

Mark all that apply.
- ❐ shopping malls
- ❐ downtown shops
- ❐ speciality shops
- ❐ import shops
- ❐ department stores
- ❐ convenience stores
- ❐ discount stores
- ❐ mail order houses
- ❐ factory discount stores
- ❐ membership discount stores
- ❐ television shopping network
- ❐ supermarkets
- ❐ from sales people calling at my door
- ❐ from sales people calling on the telephone
- ❐ the stores closest to home
- ❐ the places with the best quality
- ❐ the places with the best price
- ❐ the places with the best service

Think for a moment, then briefly list, by name, the places where you most frequently do your buying.

_____

_____

_____

_____

_____

_____

_____

_____

Now ask yourself the following questions for each of the names that you have just listed.

❐ Am I satisfied with the quality that I am buying?

❐ Am I satisfied with the service that I am receiving?

❐ Am I satisfied with the price that I am paying?

If you answered "no" to any of these questions, then you might need to look for somewhere else to buy.

Why do you buy?

❐ necessities of life

❐ personal likes and desires

❐ influence of friends

❐ influence of relatives

❐ improve self image

❐ to cheer up my spirits

❐ like to be the first to have new and innovative products

❐ can't pass on a good sale

❐ advertisements spark my interest

❐ because I work hard and deserve everything I can get

❐ sometimes impulse, not really sure

Before buying, do you take just a moment to ask yourself the simple question: "Do I really need it?"
❏ yes, most of the time
❏ no, not too often
❏ sometimes, depends on the purchase

Do you take the time to inquire about the reputation of a product or company before making large purchases?
❏ yes, most of the time
❏ no, not that often
❏ sometimes, depends on the product or company

How often do you experience "Buyer's Remorse;" the wish that you had not purchased a certain item, for it failed to deliver your expectations?
❏ all too often
❏ not very often
❏ once in a while

Have you ever gone into debt to buy something that you really didn't need?
❏ all too often
❏ no, never
❏ yes, on occasion

How do you buy?

Most people will use all of the methods listed below.
❏ cash
❏ credit cards
❏ personal check
❏ credit finance *(example: car or furniture payments)*

Do you use credit cards for record keeping and convenience, avoiding interest charges by paying the balance monthly, particularly now that the annual interest expense cannot be claimed as a tax deduction?
❐ yes, most assuredly
❐ no, I'm still trying to dig out
❐ haven't really thought about it

Did you know that many merchants actually prefer cash versus a personal check or credit card, and may be willing to offer a discount to the cash customer?
❐ yes, of course
❐ no, I didn't know that
❐ never thought about it until just now

When items that you use all of the time *(example: grocery/personal health care)* **are well below their normal price, do you have enough money to take advantage of the savings, therefore buying more than just for your short term immediate needs?**
❐ yes, every time
❐ sometimes, if I have the extra money
❐ seldom, if ever

Recognize your buying self

After you have answered the questions and identified your current buying behavior, you may see some things that you like/dislike along with some behavior traits that may even surprise you. **The whole purpose is to make you consciously aware of the who, what, when, where, why, and how of buying.**

Even if you are content and satisfied with your buying behavior, you still can fine tune it. But for most people, this may be the time to seriously consider making some changes or improvements.

CHAPTER TWO

Getting the Most
Bang for Your Buck

Buying right in the 1990s with cash

The '80s were characterized as a time of better living through leverage (borrowing to the hilt). We saw more very expensive homes being built, more luxury cars being introduced, more millionaires and billionaires being listed than ever before, and we were formally introduced to the grand artist of deal making, Mr. Donald Trump.

Who leveraged? Everyone: homeowners, corporations, and (at the head of the class) our government. Now, as a result, we face the biggest financial debacle in history as we try to dig out of the savings and loan crisis and its related effects of over leverage. All of a sudden, lenders now fear high leverage. I wonder why?!

The focus for lending money in the '90s will be specifically directed upon the borrower's ability to be able to repay the loan, regardless of what the corporation or the individual's house might be worth in a liquidation sale. The days of financing a home with a 5 percent down payment may soon be over, as we currently see real estate dropping in values in many cities across the United States. The upside-down effect is being felt; that is, having property worth less in the market than what is owed to a lender.

This change in lenders' thinking will definitely drive changes throughout our whole financial system. Will the companies and the people that have a strong cash position have the advantage in the '90s? Without a doubt! A new generation of winners and losers is starting to evolve.

The '90s will be a price driven economy

You may not have noticed because it has been slowly happening over the past few years, but the retail industry is experiencing a huge fire sale. "What?" you say. Take a moment and think about it.

Doesn't it seem as if everyone is having a sale all the time? The consumer market place has been hit so hard with sales, rebates, coupons, and discounts, that many people believe that they are not getting a good deal unless they can buy it with a rebate, coupon, or on sale.

Caveat Emptor *(let the buyer beware)*

The old maxim of "Caveat Emptor" will experience a new popularity in the '90s. Why is that, you might ask? Read on....

FURNITURE STORES ASKED TO STOP DECEPTIVE ADVERTISEMENTS

A recent article in a Northwest business journal reported that some furniture retailers were being asked by the Better Business Bureau to stop deceptive advertising on their mattress sales. Specific retailers were asked to substantiate claims of savings off regular prices, especially those claiming "half price off." Half price off of what? The regular price! What is the regular price?

Conventional thinking would say that the regular selling price is a price that exists for a certain period of time prior to the sale, and the sale should be for a shorter time than when the product was offered at the regular price. RIGHT!?

Some of the heated questions that consumers will be asking in the '90s are as follows:

- HOW DO I KNOW THAT THIS IS A FAIR AND HONEST PRICE?
- HOW DO I KNOW THAT THIS IS NOT A PHONY "SALE" RESULTING FROM INFLATED MARK-UPS?
- WHAT IS THE REAL PRICE?

Intelligent buying decisions

To become a winner at making good cash deals, you must first make an intelligent buying decision. Therefore, you must take a look at **the who, what, when, where, why, and how of buying**, but from a different perspective; that is, a perspective that may help condition your buying habits, possibly reduce your debt, and result in a little less stress in your life.

Compare what you read in this section to your Buying Self identified in chapter one.

Who to buy from?

Who are the people that you should be doing business with and why? The answer is obvious. Do business with the people that you feel you can establish confidence in and who can give you the most competitive price.

The following guidelines can help you identify these people

Look for credibility

Does the person selling the merchandise demonstrate the following characteristics:

* A comfortable ability to explain features, functions, capabilities and applications, along with a knowledge of the product's history and serviceability.
* An expressed (shown) concern to satisfy your individual needs.
* The ability to establish confidence that could possibly generate repeat and/or referral business from you.

Look for authority when cash dealing

Does the salesperson have the authority to make the best deal? This is often demonstrated with high cost items where price is often negotiated, such as: automobiles, appliances, furniture, carpeting, etc.

The best way to determine this authority is to just simply ask the question, "Do you have the authority to negotiate price?" You will get one of the following answers: yes, no, don't know, or the company sets the prices which are not negotiable. At that point, you will determine what to do. You can start to deal by offering a price that you feel is fair for the product; if the answer is no, then you should feel comfortable asking to talk with someone who does have the authority to deal on price. If prices are not negotiable for cash, and you think that they should be, then it's time to shop elsewhere.

Avoid buying as a result of pressure or from a sense of obligation

You should always be able to completely say "no" to salespeople (even if they are friends or relatives) and not be embarrassed to walk away. If they get mad as a result, then let that be their problem and not yours. REMEMBER: IF YOU DON'T THINK THAT THE DEAL IS RIGHT, WALK!

Develop good relationships with the people with whom you regularly do business

Do not be shy to tell these people why you enjoy doing business with them, or when their service has been exceptionally good. That's simple politics! If you are a cash paying customer, you will usually receive prompt attention and most often a bit of preferred treatment.

When you have been stung...

If you have been dealt with unfairly or believe that the merchandise was inferior, then make it known to the people that can do something about it. That is, when you have a legitimate complaint, most honest business owners/managers want to know about it. When a customer does not return because of product or service dissatisfaction, a business suffers. National surveys have accounted for approximately 15 percent product dissatisfaction and approximately 70 percent poor service from company employees as the primary reasons for customers not returning. Businesses work hard to attract new customers and in trying to retain existing ones. So if you professionally present your complaint to the person that is in a position to do something about it, you will probably be fairly compensated. If not, then register your complaint with the Better Business Bureau in your community or the Consumer Affairs Office in your state.

What to buy?

What should you be buying? The answer is obvious: buy all the things that you need and want which are within your budget. I emphasize "your budget" because it is critical for successful cash buying in the '90s. You must have a disciplined budget in order to generate the cash needed to do a cash deal.

When you decide you are going to buy something, buy the best. That's right, THE BEST! Remember "the best" does not always mean the most expensive. What is the best, really? When you boil it down, the best is what usually meets an individual's needs. Thus, there is a feeling of contentment when one can say, "I got the best deal on the best product for me."

Therefore, it is extremely important to develop a profile of your real need before trying to fill it. One way to do this would be to make a brief description of just what you think it will take to satisfy you in (as is often said) "getting the job done." This is a practice that professional buyers for big businesses follow regularly, only they refer to it as writing the specifications. This is a way of organizing just what is needed and avoiding under or over buying.

Think about it for a minute. You wouldn't seriously consider buying fine expensive clothing to work in the garden, nor would you buy a luxury car to haul lumber (even though we may know of some people that have done these things and many more just as seemingly ridiculous—surely not us).

A good buy means nothing if it's not the right product to "get the job done!"

Why do so many people misbuy in relation to their needs? This question could probably be answered with a number of reasonably good answers, but for the most part when people misbuy, they are usually not fully conscious of what they are doing. Therefore, they continually run the risk of never getting the full use or value from many of the things they buy. Worse, they can later wind-up suffering from BUYER'S REMORSE. Yes, wishing that they had never bought it, often too late or at a great expense, if the item in question is big ticket.

Another pitfall is THE EMOTIONAL BUY . . . falling in love with it at the store or in the showroom.

The following story is a personal experience that saved us a few thousand dollars and a lot of frustration.

When it was time to replace our family car, my sons and I were very interested in buying a van. My wife was firmly opposed to the idea, for no other reason than she just didn't like them. Well, the more I looked at them, the more I was convinced that we definitely needed one. Plus, everyone I had talked to that owned a van had only positive things to say. (Then again, remembering that when most people make a buying mistake, they usually don't like to talk about it). In my mind, it was almost settled, and my wife would learn to like it, right? WRONG!

I cooled my emotionalism and fell back upon my professional buying skills and began the analysis process. Our needs were easy to identify:
• Seating capacity for five.
• All the standard and luxury features that would be available on most vehicles.

- Generous cargo capacity was important for our needs, along with being able to have privacy and security that would be found in the normal automobile trunk.
- Enjoyable driving, something comfortable and fun.
- Finally, whatever we bought needed to be within our budget...THAT WAS FIRM.

We wanted the most for our dollars in fulfilling our needs...the basic quest of most buyers. But I had to get the emotionalism out of the deal. My wife wouldn't change her mind and neither would I, and there didn't appear to be any room for compromise. So we rented a van for a few days, and that made all the difference in helping us make our decision.

Vans are great, and perhaps some day we will own one, but for now we have a sedan with every luxury option available. It's perfect for our family needs and most importantly, we are ALL enjoying it.

To have purchased a van equipped with the same features would have been out of our budget. We refused to go over that amount, so our choice was a minimally equipped model. Knowing my family and myself, we all would have had a severe case of "buyers remorse" within a few weeks; especially after having read an article in a business journal that specifically stated that vans were generating a $5,000 per unit profit over the normal profit for that manufacturer. "Why?," the article asked, "Because vans have been so popular that the manufacturers and dealers can get the price."

I hope that after reading this story you will recognize the importance of analyzing value and in determining specifications and features that will adequately satisfy your needs, and in staying within your budget.

The following guidelines can help you in determining what to buy

Analyze value

You must determine whether the cost is equal to fulfilling your need and use.

Ask yourself the following questions:
• Are all the features of the product really needed? What is their purpose and do they suit your needs?
• What is the total price, and the specific price for each optional feature?
• What is the history of the product? The reputation, guarantee/warranty, serviceability, and how long is the guarantee or the product expected to last?
• How do any alternative products compare?
• Does it represent the best deal for you?

Determine specifications or features

Specifically identify exactly what you want to buy. If you do not know precisely what you want, then you may find yourself trusting the advice or judgment of a salesperson, which may not always be in your best interest.

Do your homework

Begin with a pencil and notepad and simply write out what you think you want and need. Then, make a complete list of questions that you would like to have answered. This will help establish the framework for you to set the balance between quality, price, and suitability. When available, product brochures are most helpful.

Some of the questions that you may ask are as follows:
• Has the government established a market grade or standard?
• What is the reputation of the manufacturer's brand name, when it comes to quality and service?

- Has the specific industry established set standards for quality, workmanship and testing methods? An example would be UL Approved (Underwriters Laboratory) for electrical products.
- Are there any performance standards? This is clearly demonstrated with the automobile industry.
- Where can a sample be seen, examined and tested?

This process would be used when buying things like televisions, VCRs, compact disc players, washers/dryers, telephones, microwaves, cameras, carpeting, etc; anything and everything that represents a substantial value investment for you.

One of the best sources to consult is *Consumer Reports*, published by Consumers Union, a nonprofit organization with no commercial ties. Along with their monthly magazine, a yearly buying guide is published that compares the value and performance of the most used products and services in the market place.

When to buy?

When is the best time to buy anything? That answer will vary according to what you are buying and the urgency of your need.

Some guidelines to follow for knowing when to buy

A good rule to remember is "never buy anything in haste."

Try to be careful not to jump into deals as a result of a newspaper ad or a radio or television commercial which emphasizes urgency to buy during the special sale at a limited time offer. Although these advertisements may provide information on exactly what you need or might want, don't lose sight of the fact that their purpose is to motivate you to promptly respond. You, the buyer, should be intelligently acting upon advertisements, as opposed to emotionally reacting to a sensational ad presentation. *NOTE: While buying in haste should be avoided, be careful not to be over cautious. In some situations, if you wait too long, you may miss a good sale on the item you need.*

Learn how the stores in your community price and merchandise

Take the time to learn how the stores that you frequently patronize conduct business. *Try to answer the following questions about each store:*

* When are new products put on the shelves or on display, what day of the week or month, and at what usual time of the day? If it's a grocery store, think about when you see the best selection of meats and produce at the best prices.
* When do sales or price reductions take place: the first, middle, or end of the week, month or season?

If possible, wait for prices to cool off

When products are hot as a result of new or improved technology or because of a style change, their prices are usually higher. We also see this with seasonal items such as clothing, lawn mowers, ski equipment, toys, etc.

Most of the time, we think of these things only when we need them. But by planning ahead in anticipation of our needs, we could save in the off seasons when merchants are usually anxious to deal...ESPECIALLY FOR CASH!

What about technology? Remember pocket calculators, VCRs, digital watches and home computers (just to mention a few). These products were all very high priced when they were initially introduced to the market place. But as technology improved and consumer demand increased, prices became lower and very competitive. We are currently seeing that happen with cellular telephones; prices are dropping for the actual phones as well as for the cellular network service. A few items that are still hot (high priced) in the 1990s are big screen televisions and compact disc players. If you can plan ahead and maintain a patient attitude, you will save.

Where to buy?

Where are the best places to buy?

The answer is easy. The best places to buy are the places that can consistently meet your needs with the right quality and service at a fair competitive price. Therefore, you must first be able to recognize how quality and price affect you.

What does quality mean to you?

By definition, quality is that which each individual identifies as being suitable in fulfilling a particular purpose or need. Quality may be identified by:
   a. brand name
   b. reputation
   c. consistency
   d. grade
   e. looking at a sample or demonstration

What does a fair (competitive) price mean to you?

That question may have many interpretations, but typically a fair price is when the person buying and the person selling are both satisfied that the price is fair. The buyer, of course, would like that price to be the lowest possible.

Guidelines for choosing where to buy

Evaluate the places where you are currently buying
Ask yourself the following questions:

• Do I get the best values for the prices that I pay?
• Have the salespeople always been courteous and helpful?
• Has the service after the sale been good, especially with products that need service or adjustment?
• Have my overall past experiences been favorable?
• Would I feel comfortable in recommending the place to friends?

If you answered "no" to any of these questions, then you need to consider buying somewhere else.

Recognize the signs of a good place to buy
They are as follows:

• Always competitively priced.
• Always offering your kind of quality backed by excellent service.
• Always has friendly, cooperative and helpful salespeople that put forth the extra effort to satisfy.
• Always willing to exchange or accept returned merchandise.

Consider the buying expense

All the costs involved when buying an item must be evaluated. *Some typical costs that are often overlooked when buying are as follows:*

• The price of gasoline when driving distance is involved.
• Personal time taken to drive or look for an item.
• Long distance telephoning to inquire as to out of town prices and/or when ordering.
• Mailing/shipping when buying from out of town.
• Service, installation or delivery when service or installation are not included in the selling price.

When making the final buying decision as to where to buy, take the time to total all the related expenses which will represent the true cost of the item. It may be cheaper to drive across town, order from a catalog, or pay for installation and service, or it might cost more in the final analysis. But you will not know until you check it out.

Why buy?

Why do you buy the things that you do, probably for a number of very good reasons and maybe for a few that are not so good? But, whatever your reasons have been, you should now be asking yourself the following questions before buying:

• Can I really afford it?
• Will it adequately meet my needs?
• Can I justify it?

If you can answer "yes" to the three questions, then you should feel satisfied with your buying decisions. But the answer to the question, "Can I justify it?" may be new to many people, because during the '80s there didn't seem to be much justification for a lot of purchases. This is evidenced by the high degree of consumer spending and tremendous increase in the amount of personal consumer debt, as well as growth of the U.S. Government's debt.

"Can I justify it?" will be a popular question being asked by many consumers in the '90s if they want to survive or build a cash reserve.

Can I justify it?
(I mean me)

For many years, I have enjoyed wearing a particular brand of shoes. I bought my first pair in 1969 for $45, which was expensive for that year. Since that time, that

same pair of shoes now (in 1993) sells for $265. Guess
what? I can't justify that price, but I still like the shoes
and am not happy with any other kind. So, what's the
answer? I bought a pair for summer, last December, from
a fine department store chain's discount rack store for
half price. That was a good deal and I could justify it.

Some guidelines to think about why you buy

Define your buying objective

*This can be accomplished by asking yourself the
following questions:*

• What will buying the item do for me (or my family)?
• Will buying the item represent a good investment,
either monetarily or for personal pleasure?
• Should I buy a quality that will last or something that
is cheaper and will just get me through a short period
of time?

A good example is when deciding to buy clothing
(personal or for the kids). There is a wide choice and price
range. The answer of course, will depend upon your
buying objective.

Consider renting, when applicable

Today, almost every community has a Rent-All
business that will rent virtually everything from A to Z.
So, before buying something that you may occasionally
use, consider renting.

A good example might be that of a motor home. Can
you really justify the investment, insurance and
maintenance costs if you will only use it a few times a
year for short trips!? Do the homework and calculate the
costs versus renting a motor home by the day, week or
month. The list of examples is endless.

Think about doing it yourself, if possible

Never lose sight of the fact that you might be able to do it yourself and save. More and more manufacturers are gearing their products for the fast growing do-it-yourself market. This, along with the abundance of "how to" books, makes the idea of doing it yourself very encouraging.

Before making the decision whether to do it yourself or hire it out, you must first ask yourself a few questions such as:

• Do I have the time to spend and the necessary equipment to do the job?
• Do I have the confidence in my abilities?
• Will I be satisfied with the quality when I am finished?
• Are there any additional items or skills needed that I might not know about?
• How much money will I really save?

You might very well be able to do some plumbing, electrical work and simple auto mechanics, just to mention a few. Intelligently weigh the facts, then make a decision. *NOTE: We will see many people in the '90s actually building their own homes and saving thousands of dollars in the process.*

How to buy in the '90s

How should you be doing your buying in the '90s? The answer is simple; with the skills of a professional buyer and CASH. The skills of a professional buyer can be learned and effectively used in every buying situation.

THE POWER OF CASH DEALS

N O T E

The following chapters of this book explain professional buying skills and techniques that you will be able to immediately implement into your everyday buying behavior. The results should be reflected with some definite cash savings to you.

CHAPTER THREE

Twenty-One Cash Negotiating Tips

1. Make sure that you are talking to the right person

This person should be the one who can make the deal or negotiate the price. Don't be shy in asking, "Are you the boss, owner, manager; the person that I can talk with regarding a cash price?" Otherwise, you may be somewhat embarrassed by jumping into a cash negotiating position with someone who can do nothing to help you, and may not even understand what you are attempting to accomplish. (Refer to page 27, Look for Authority When Cash Dealing).

2. Never feel guilty about asking for a lower price when offering cash

Learn to overcome the basic fear of rejection by keeping in mind the worse that can happen is to be told "no" to your cash offer. You can always calmly say "thanks anyway" and pay the selling price or walk away if you think that price is not fair.

3. Don't try to negotiate a cash price over the telephone

Negotiating for cash pricing may only work if the person specifically remembers you from previous dealings or purchases, otherwise, you will most likely not be taken serious. The key factors in negotiating a cash price are timing, moods, expressions of confidence, and integrity along with face to face dealing.

4. Look and act professional

Your personal presentation can make the critical difference as to whether or not you are taken seriously. So, be confident and optimistic in your attitude, and neat and mannered in your appearance. You are a serious cash buyer.

5. Always be yourself

Never act out of character nor as a tough or authoritative type. This action could be interpreted as an immediate put-down. Being full of smiles is also not the way to present a cash offer. You want to be yourself in a pleasant and serious mood, with clear and concise language in making your request for a lower price in consideration for an immediate cash payment.

6. Identify personality traits and sort out key facts

When dealing with a seller, always ask yourself what logically makes sense and what is nonsense. Over time and with practice and experience, this will become easier. Once the personality that you will be dealing with and the facts are clearly set forth, then cash negotiation can be a simple routine.

7. Dealing with the fast talker

Take control and slow down the speed, otherwise you will be pushed into paying a higher price. The elements to remember are seriousness, calmness, and being in control. Fast talkers can easily confuse the negotiation and leave you frustrated. They also often spark personality conflicts which can create an argumentative situation. So, keep emotions in check and do not allow intimidation to creep into your cash dealing.

8. Dealing with the casual seller

The person who seems not to care at all if the merchandise sells and doesn't appear to show an ounce of anxiousness in wanting to deal for cash should never be taken for granted. Make a cash offer in the same casual manner, for you could just as easily be doing business with someone else.

9. Dealing with the "Trust Me" person

This is a person who, in conversation, emphasizes a high personal degree of honesty and integrity along with a proud reputation; implying a subtle resentment when questions about price, quality or service are raised. This is a form of gentle intimidation. So, present yourself as a competent person who always exercises thoroughness in checking out details. Then present your cash offer. *Note: Use caution after the deal with the "Trust Me" person!*

The "Trust Me" person may offer to sell you extras or add-ons to the product in order to generate additional revenue after the deal. The "Trust Me" person will often present these items for your serious consideration because, after all, this person had your best interest at heart... and perhaps your confidence too. Remember: Keep thinking logically!

10. Dealing with the strong silent type

The strong silent type is the person who listens to your cash price offer and does not respond, or simply says very little with no indication of either agreement or disagreement. This style represents a smooth way of throwing the pressure back to you. Respond with similar silence, for you have stated your cash offer and have no need to further explain, other than a final inquiry as to the acceptance or rejection of your cash offer.

11. Dealing with a flatterer

The flatterer is a master of compliments, a person who skillfully hooks egos with flattering remarks aimed to please and pump up spirits. Comments that are directed toward your shrewdness, keen intellect, pride and perhaps status. Statements like: "You could turn around and sell this tomorrow and make money;" "You are a born wheeler-dealer;" "Your friends and neighbors will really be impressed;" "You'll be among the elite;" or "Don't tell anyone that I'm giving you this special cash price." All these types of statements are designed with one result in mind: to leave you with a feeling of power or superiority. Remember: it's only bait!

Note: The flatterer may suggest taking a break from the negotiating to have a drink or pie and coffee. The saying of "mixing a little business with pleasure" applies here. Don't! Finish the deal, for the social aspect can add confusion and result in your paying more than necessary.

12. Dealing with family, friends, or neighbors

This can be dangerous for all the reasons that one can imagine. Most people, when asked about doing business with family, friends, or neighbors seem to usually have a story to tell relating to a less-than-positive experience.

Often this dealing leads to ruining, or at the very least, straining a relationship. **Caution: Think logically, not emotionally. Let your good judgment prevail, regardless of how good or harmless the deal may look.**

CONSULTING FAMILY AND FRIENDS

To seek sound advice from the people that intimately know your tastes, preferences and objectives can be valuable. They can provide valid input to help you make critical buying decisions. If they don't really know you, the result will only be their expressed opinions, based upon their own perspectives which could leave you confused and frustrated. As your experience increases, your ability to clearly and logically think independently will also increase.

13. Dealing with the warm seller

The warm seller is the new friend who says, "Let's get together, we have a lot in common." The friend who is quick to do favors with no apparent pay back, although is building a relationship of confidence and trust for the warm sell. The warm seller is frequently involved in leadership positions within clubs, social, and church organizations; therefore positioned as a person of confidence and trust.

Your business is always subtly solicited. It is easy to become too embarrassed to check or compare cash prices, because, the warm seller appears to be your friend. This ploy is the selfish motive of many people involved in multi-level marketing programs that involve cosmetics, home products, investments and insurance. Again, think logically and not emotionally; let your good judgment prevail.

Caution: One or two negative experiences can easily and quickly allow your attitude to become cynical. Remember, there are a lot of genuinely sincere people with kind hearts and righteous motives that are not "Warm Sellers." Conscious experience over time will help you to be able to promptly identify them.

14. Dealing with the Good Guy /Bad Guy routine

This routine is where the seller assumes the role of being your friend [the good guy] and wants to make the sale at your cash price; but he must deal with his sales manager or boss [the bad guy] who wants "more." In so doing, the good guy asks you to raise your offer to appease the bad guy. This can go back and forth several times until they believe that they had squeezed you as much as possible. This is the technique typically used in automobile sales.

Rule: Don't play the game! Stick to your cash offer, and if it is refused don't be afraid to walk. Don't be surprised if you see them chasing after you, this time ready to negotiate on your terms.

15. Develop listening skills

Train yourself to concentrate and effectively listen for the facts and realities of every deal. Learn to recognize when someone is not telling you the truth. Don't be afraid to just walk out on a bold-face lie. Some examples would be as follows: "If you don't buy right now, we cannot guarantee you this price later;" "The lender says that you have to buy the extended warranty;" "By law, we have to add a 5 percent delivery charge;" or "You will be able to get the full amount back on your taxes." Depending upon the exact circumstances there might be an element of truth in any one of these statements. But if you know for certain that there is absolutely no truth to a statement, don't be shy in asking for proof. If it's not available, you probably will not be happy doing business with that establishment.

16. Sometimes a ridiculous offer makes sense

When you sense that a seller may have a real need to sell, a ridiculous offer tests the degree of that need to sell. You will then recognize just how anxious, how hungry of a position the seller may be in. The seller may need to make bonus sales, achieve sales goals or just plain business survival. If the ridiculous cash offer is accepted, be careful not to act surprised, and always present the cash offer in a manner that makes sense.

For example: A name brand watch has a retail price of $295. You look it over and it fits your needs; then you simply state the facts to the jewelry store owner or manager: "I love the watch, but all I have to spend is a flat $200 in cash. Therefore, I guess I'll have to pass it up for now, because I'm not really interested in any other model or make of watch." That may be the end of it, or the manager may be ringing up the sale for $200 cash. This situation is not uncommon with merchandise that is often discounted 20 to 40 percent.

17. The flat take-it-or-leave-it price

THERE ARE THREE BASIC RESPONSES TO THE TAKE-IT-OR-LEAVE-IT PRICE:

1. **Take it.** Pay the price when your good judgment tells you it is fair.
2. **Leave it.** Walk away because, in your judgment, the price is too high and you can do better shopping around.
3. **Negotiate with cash and possible trade-offs.** Most often, the take-it-or-leave-it price is firm in the seller's mind. Therefore, trying to hammer the price down will usually result in frustration and a possible argument. However, visibly showing cash could change the mood. It is worth the try! If it doesn't work, quickly change

the conversation by asking questions about the product (additional features, other applications, available colors, warranty coverage, etc). This could possibly open the door for trade-offs such as picking up an extra option with no price increase, whereby the seller is willing to throw something in. You are simply demonstrating your flexibility in deal-making.

An example of trade-offs would be when buying a camera. The base price for the model is a flat take-it-or-leave-it. This would be the situation when the camera is priced the same at all the leading authorized retailers. But, you may possibly succeed in getting a few extras like a lens filter, upgraded carrying case, or other accessories. Present the seller with a few "what if's" and "what about's," show the cash and see what happens.

18. When it's the cheapest price in town

When buying from the cheapest priced place in town, be cautious! If the seller is positioned to just grab the bucks without building a loyal customer base of satisfied customer references, make certain that you ask the right questions in checking out the details. Don't worry about taking the time or be too embarrassed to inquire as to the product's serviceability, warranty, etc. Avoid, or at least reduce the potential for problems or additional costs and expenses related to the product once you have it home.

19. The best cash deal

Does your cash deal have the look and smell of fairness? Is it fair to you and equally fair to the seller; a 50-50 you win/seller wins versus a 60-40 you win/seller loses? Remember, both parties need to win. The selfish "beat 'em up" buyer is never appreciated, nor is that the reputation that compliments one's character. You need to be able to save a little money and the seller needs to be able to make a fair profit to survive in business and allow you to feel good about the deal so that you will become a regular customer.

Note: Never ask for a volume price quotation when in fact you only intend to buy one or two units of the item.

20. Don't kiss and tell

Professional buyers don't brag about their good deals. Professionals also don't drop names in an attempt to impress their friends or associates at work. A bit of self control and discipline is necessary following the typical excitement associated after closing a good deal. Caution is necessary when deciding who to confide in and who might be listening at the next table or in the elevator. Avoid any possibility of embarrassment.

21. Be careful not to out-smart yourself

Cash deals are plentiful during these economic times, and very inviting as prices are drastically reduced. But be careful that emotional impulses do not out-weigh your common sense, good judgment and logical thinking. Take inventory, check your garage, basement, attic, and closets for items once purchased and seldom, if ever used. You certainly won't need to add to them.

NEGOTIATING

For many nations of the world, price negotiating has always been a strong part of the culture as a way of life and a way of conducting business.

CHAPTER FOUR

Getting Out of Debt and Creating Cash

Personal debt does not occur overnight. Therefore, getting out of debt will tend to be a slow and, in some cases, a painful process. It is like the individual who wakes up one morning and decides to lose 20 pounds in order to become healthier and more physically fit. The faithful dieter or jogger knows that a daily commitment is required in order to achieve the weight goal accompanied by the healthier feelings. Such is the case with the financial money manager/budgeter. The task will not be easy. Recognize that getting out of debt is not impossible, but will require self discipline in order to achieve and maintain a healthy financial balance.

To get started immediately, consider the following steps:

1. Prepare and organize a yearly household budget that is tight, but realistic. Identify old, current and anticipated expenses. Then evaluate where the money goes and where you will be able to cut back. Determine what you can comfortably afford and spend no more. (Refer to page 60, Know Your Debt Level.)

2. Establish a defined payment schedule for all debt; mortgage payment, auto payment, installment contracts, credit cards, etc. Avoid the human tendency to pay only the minimum due each month.

3. Think through all future purchases. When possible, avoid creating new debt. If credit cards are a problem, cut them up, pay off and close the accounts, and remove the temptations.

4. Start saving regularly!! Remove any possible temptation not to save by setting up an automatic withdrawal taken out of your paycheck or checking account to be placed in a savings account. The idea is to pay yourself first; 10 or 15 percent of your gross earnings could be a goal to set forth. Along with paying off debt, it is important to have a cash reserve for emergencies. (Refer to page 88, Statement Savings Account).

5. If you own a home, consider a home equity loan or refinancing as a way of consolidating your debt or to fund a one time expense (such as the purchase of a car, to pay off medical bills, college tuition, or for home improvements).

NOTE: Above all else, do not use the cash equity from your home for consumer spending or vacation travel.

Home Equity Loans create quick cash

Home Equity Loans are rapidly gaining in popularity, and if you have owned a home for even a short period of time, you may qualify for a home equity loan. You must have a good income producing job with reasonably sound employment status in order to qualify; just as you did with your original mortgage loan.

Home Equity Loans are available in two versions

1. A lump sum loan to you in the form of a check to spend as you see fit.

2. A line of credit. A checkbook is issued to you for your convenience in writing checks against the line of credit. Once you write a check, the line of credit is activated and then you will be on a monthly repayment schedule for that amount plus interest. As you write more checks, the amount of your payment will increase.

The Home Equity Loan works as follows

Say that you purchased your home in 1980 for $100,000, with a $10,000 down payment and a $90,000 mortgage. By 1993, the value of the home has become $165,000 (as per bank appraisal) which increases your equity to at least $75,000 or more (depending on your original mortgage loan). This amount is the equity portion upon which a lender will make a home equity loan.

The loan typically can be for as much as 75 to 80 percent of that equity balance. So, if the balance was $75,000 and you had the income to make the loan payments, you could qualify for a $60,000 (80%) Home Equity Loan. In effect, you are pulling $60,000 cash out of your home. Also, you should be able to position yourself to take immediate advantage of tax deductible interest payments which the Internal Revenue Service allows for home loans.

The terms and conditions of Home Equity Loans are just as variable and competitive as home mortgage loans. Therefore, a prudent effort to shop around and check out all the details of a loan can lead to saving many dollars over the term of the loan. Watch for details such as: fixed or adjustable rates (if adjustable, the maximum cap rate must be known); costs (including loan fees, appraisal fee, title insurance, etc); also, as home values fall in some parts of the country, some lenders require home equity borrowers to promptly pay back portions to the principal of their loans, as well as interest, so that the loan is always in line with the current value of the home.

Refinancing

Refinancing a home loan can be another excellent way to reduce debt or to pull out some cash. Whatever the plan may be a few guidelines should be considered:

1. The interest rate should be at least two percentage points lower than what you are paying currently.

2. Plan to live in the home for at least three more years in order to recoup refinancing fees.

3. Get the most for your money. Rates often fluctuate from lender to lender and from day to day. Shop around to get the most without having to pay a lot of fees.

NOTE: Seriously consider a 15 year mortgage. The monthly payment is usually only 20 to 30 percent above payments on a 30 year mortgage because more of each monthly payment goes toward principal instead of interest. The savings are tremendous (consult a payment schedule) and will result in getting you out of debt sooner.

Be careful... don't bet the whole farm!!!

A Home Equity Loan or refinancing can create some quick cash, but is not designed to be a buffer against recession. For safety's sake, always leave yourself a cash reserve cushion in the event that a disaster hits. A home is a terrible thing to lose. The chilling fact is that there is a tremendous amount of foreclosed properties nationwide that are owned by the Government Resolution Trust Corporation as a direct result of the Savings and Loan Crisis.

The financially overextended

According to the Administrative Office of U.S. Courts, 718,107 personal bankruptcies were recorded during 1990. This record high number is a result of large consumer debt loads, tough economic times and the increased acceptance of bankruptcy as a way out of financial burdens. The large consumer debt loads came as a result of being financially overextended; through over spending, over borrowing and then encountering unexpected reversals such as income reduction, medical bills, or even job loss. In many cases, debts, not including rent or mortgage payments, exceeded personal net income.

If these circumstances vaguely describe your current situation, STOP EVERYTHING! Take control of your finances now. Don't let your finances control you.

Immediately take the following steps:

1. If you are in total doubt as to what to do next, seek professional help. Financial counseling centers are in most communities and are rapidly increasing in numbers.

2. Consolidate your debts and go on a total cash basis for all of your buying until your problem is brought under control.

3. Manage your money and your spending by learning to live beneath your means and spending less than you earn.

Know your debt level

Check your current financial picture by completing the following two worksheets:

CURRENT RATIO

1. From your pay stubs add up your monthly gross pay adding any additional income to that figure.
   Enter the total here: A. $_____
2. Compile all your montly credit, installment and consumer loan payments (rent/morgage payment).
   Enter the total here: B. $_____
   Current Ratio:
   Divide B. by A. x 100   _____%

The **Current Ratio** should not exceed 20 to 25 percent for the average person or family; 36 percent if rent or mortgage payments are included. According to financial consultants, these are the ratios that represent a comfortable debt level. However, accurately determining a "true" comfortable debt level will depend upon your individual spending habits.

NOTE: If you are in the habit of spending a lot of cash on entertainment, sports, lunches, etc., then you should plan to have a lower ratio, such as 10 to 15 percent excluding rent or mortgage payments.

The second worksheet provides a broader look at all the debts that you have accumulated to date as compared to all your assets. The **Debt Ratio** will help you to see how your current debt impacts your future. Again, the same ratios apply; 20 to 25 percent if rent or mortgage payment is not included.

DEBT RATIO

(date): _____

ASSETS

Cash/Checking/Savings Accts $	_____
CD's, Stocks & Bonds	_____
Home	_____
Business	_____
Loans to others	_____
IRA's and Annuities	_____
Autos	_____
Antiques & Jewelry	_____
Other	_____
Total Assets	**C.** _____

LIABILITIES

Rent	_____
Utilities/Taxes	_____
Medical bills	_____
Credit balances	_____
Home mortgage	_____
Auto/Home/Personal loans	_____
Insurance premiums	_____
Other	_____
Total Liabilities	**D.** _____

DEBT RATIO:

Divide D. by C. x 100 _____ %

Finally...if you do not like what you see on the charts and would like help in financial planning, contact a local credit management organization or call Consumer Credit Counseling Service at (800) 388-2227. These nonprofit counseling services are there to help with advice and suggestions for debt problems.

A quote worth remembering...

"There is no dignity quite so impressive, and no independence quite so important as living within your means... Any other course for me would be the senseless imitation of a fowl which was attempting to light higher than its roost."

Calvin Coolidge

CHAPTER FIVE

Car Buying:
A Cash Drain

RETHINK installment credit interest payments for car buying

During the strong economy of the '80s, wages steadily rose and many families were being supported by dual incomes. Consumers also accepted extraordinary price increases for cars. With the incoming cash flow, why shouldn't they? The only requirements were qualifying with a lender and meeting the monthly payment figure. Financing was extended to 5 and 7 years in order to allow for manageable monthly payments. Also, automobile leasing gained in popularity.

The Federal Government allowed the total interest expense to be written off on annual tax returns. Plus, new car prices were significantly rising every year. Conventional wisdom dictated that buying and financing now versus trying to save the money and pay cash made little sense; for it was next to impossible to save it fast enough to keep pace with annual price increases. Automobile inflation clearly outran bank savings (even with compound interest).

The car buying climate for the '90s presents a very different set of figures as the economic wheel of fortune has taken an abrupt spin. The Federal Government no longer allows writing off the automobile retail installment credit interest expense on annual tax returns; car prices have leveled off to some degree; and price concessions and rebates are necessary to stimulate new car sales.

How high is high?!

According to the Department of Commerce, Bureau of Labor Statistics, the average price of a new car rose from $7,574 in 1980 to $16,017 in 1990. Automakers hiked prices and buyers chose more options. The bubble appears now to have burst, news headlines report the following:

AUTOMOBILE PRODUCTION SHUTS DOWN BECAUSE SHOWROOMS ARE OVERSTOCKED

CAR AND TRUCK SALES RUN ABOUT 26.5% BEHIND LAST YEAR'S PACE

GM LOSES A LANDMARK $23.5 BILLION

TROUBLES IN AUTO INDUSTRY ARE DEEP... MULTI-MILLION DOLLAR COST CUTS TAKE PLACE

"ANALYSTS SAY A RECESSION IN THE OVERALL ECONOMY IS CAUSING A DEPRESSION IN THE AUTO INDUSTRY."

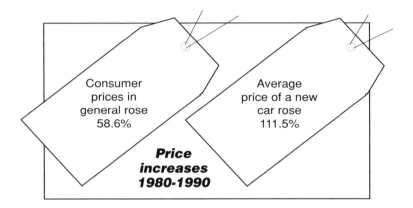

Consumer prices in general rose 58.6%

Average price of a new car rose 111.5%

Price increases 1980-1990

A look at the numbers

The following page shows a typical example of an Automobile Retail Installment Contract that is geared for a monthly payment of just under $300 for five years (the legal terms and conditions have been omitted to abbreviate the example).

RETAIL INSTALLMENT PLAN (Simple Interest)

$15,281.00 - includes sale price plus tax and all fees
- 1,200.00 - less total cash down payment (cash or trade-in vehicle)
$14,081.00 - principal balance

Annual Percentage Rate The cost of my credit as a yearly rate. 9.9%	**Finance Charge** The dollar amount the credit will cost me. $3,901.00	**Amount Financed** The amount of the credit provided me. $14,081.00	**Total Payments** The amount I will have paid after all payments. $17,982.00	**Total Sale Price** The total cost of my purchase on credit, including my down payment of $1,200.00. $19,182.00

Number of Payments   60 (5 Years)
Amount of Payments $299.70
Payment Schedule   Monthly - Beginning: (day)/(month)/(year)

SUBJECT TO CREDIT APPROVAL
CONTRACT ACCEPTED BY: *(seller)* _____

NOTICE TO BUYER • RETAIL INSTALLMENT CONTRACT
Do not sign this contract before you read it or if it contains any blank space, except that if delivery of the vehicle is to be made to you after this contract is signed, the serial number may be filled in at the time of delivery. You are entitled to a copy of this contract. You have the right to pay off in advance the full amount due if you do so you may save a portion of the finance charge. The undersigned acknowledges receipt of a completed copy of this contract and agrees to its terms.

Buyer signs _____   Date _____

During the decade of the '80s, this type of auto buying/financing made logical sense. As shown in the following example, if a car sold for $15,281 in 1980, the same car in 1985 would have been $23,800 (as per the automobile inflation rate).

1985 Price	$23,800.00
Accumulated savings/plus	
interest from 1980	-20,968.83
SHORT (less buying power)	($2,831.17)
1980 Price	$15,281.00
Finance Charge	+ 3,901.00
TOTAL COST	$19,182.00

So, in five years of normal bank statement savings, the accumulated savings and compound interest would have been $20,968.83 (see statement savings chart page 88). This would have resulted in a shortfall of $2,831.17 less buying power.

Quite simply, financing meant more buying power during this rapid inflationary period. Plus, during this time the interest expense was allowed to be declared on a Federal Income Tax Return, which provided for additional savings.

This buying power is not the case in the '90s. With rebates and other buying incentives, prices on many cars are holding the line and in some cases actually decreasing. So when an automobile manufacturer has a price increase, it is often followed by discounts.

Play it again... now in the '90s.

The car that sells for $15,281 in 1993 will probably still sell for close to that amount for the next 2 to 4 years. If the overall economy strengthens and consumer interest in new car buying increases, then prices will undoubtedly increase (and rebates and discounts will stop). But price increases will be marginal and nowhere near the 1980-1990 level. Recovery in the giant auto industry will likely be slower than in any other period of history, because there are more major manufacturers competing for business, other than just the "Big 3" (GM, Ford, Chrysler).

Plus, there will be a decreasing number of potential consumers as reflected by the dramatic decline in birth rates.

Look at the statement savings chart again (page 88) and make the same buying/financial comparisons. While it is impossible to accurately predict future car prices, a market trend has evolved and definitely reflects a reasonably sound guideline to help make the best buying decision.

A well established fact is that next to a home, the single largest investment that most people will make is the purchase of an automobile. Therefore, the selection and purchasing procedure should represent the buyer's best effort.

An investment or just plain transportation?

Whatever your buying motives may be, it is important to keep in mind that someday you will want to sell or trade what you are buying today. So, before making the final buying decision, it is important to check the resale value.

An easy way to find this value is to check the advertised market resale values in your local Sunday newspaper. Check the resale prices for the last three years of the particular vehicle that you are interested in buying. Also, check two comparable vehicles within the same price range but by different manufacturers, perhaps domestic versus imported. Another way is to check with buying services that provide automobile financial facts, such as AAA Auto Pricing Service, Car/Puter's Instant Pricing Hotline, National Auto Brokers, and Car Bargains (see page 113 for telephone numbers). Facts such as wholesale and retail new car prices, high and low used car valuations, safety features and maintenance/ repair histories should all be investigated.

	Your choice of vehicle Make/Model	Domestic comparison (similar vehicle) Make/Model	Import comparison (similar vehicle) Make/Model
1993	15,595	14,990	16,250
1992	13,850	12,500	14,795
1991	11,395	9,950	12,950

Doing this type of chart will provide you with an accurate picture of what your purchase may be worth over the next three years, given the state of the automotive market conditions in your community. Compare the resale prices to the new vehicle sticker prices being advertised in order to determine a reasonably accurate dollar depreciation. Then ponder those figures as you are making your buying decision. UPSIDE-DOWN IN A CAR is not a position that is at all comfortable, financially speaking. It specifically refers to the outstanding balance owed on the car being more than the car is actually worth in the marketplace. Simply stated, if the car had to be sold or if the car was in an accident and deemed "totalled" by the insurance company, the owner would be responsible for coming up with the cash difference to pay off the lender. This occurs when the rate of depreciation is faster than the payment pay-off schedule.

To avoid being upside-down in a car, consider the following:

1. Pay cash, if possible.

2. When financing, be sure that the cash down payment or value of the trade-in vehicle is substantial.

3. Purchase a vehicle that maintains a strong market resale value.

4. Buy a dealer demonstrator model or factory executive car with low mileage and new car warranty. These can be purchased well below new car asking prices.

5. Check with leasing companies for current year models that are for sale. These vehicles are usually well maintained and extended warranties can be purchased. Almost all of the first year's depreciation can be saved.

Steps to successfully negotiate the purchase of a car using cash

KNOWLEDGE IS POWER

A. Identify the specific vehicle that you want to purchase (year, make, model, standard and optional equipment, and color choices).

B. Recognize the market conditions and the extent of competition. The Sunday newspaper ads with price comparisons will provide a good measure.

C. Research the reputation of several automobile dealerships in terms of their fairness in deal making. Simply ask around (friends, neighbors, co-workers, etc.).

NOTE: Buying a car should represent an intelligent and mature decision.

Set the price objective

Look at both the high and low price ranges, then establish a fair market value price that you would be prepared to spend for the vehicle. The buying services discussed on page 113 can be an excellent source for specifically identifying wholesale and retail prices as well as high and low used car valuations.

Trade-in vehicle: The key word to keep in mind here is "realistic." If you want the lowest price off the sticker value for the new vehicle, then do not expect more than low wholesale book for your trade-in vehicle. The best situation is with "no trade," which can happen for the first time buyer or person who is able to successfully sell his/her existing vehicle (typically accomplished with a line ad in the local newspaper). Buying "clean" without a trade is obviously the best position, but is not always possible.

A comment on financing

Thoroughly assess your financial situation. Retail installment credit financing may represent the best choice, given your individual circumstances. But after having checked all the alternatives (such as a personal line of credit, home equity loan, etc.) remember the previously stated suggestions on how not to be upside-down in a car.

Cash gives greater bargaining strength

The ability to write a personal check or to have a cashier's check made out to yourself (only needing your endorsement with the name of the dealership to be negotiable) represents "instant cash" to the dealer. The psychological message that becomes loud and clear is that you are a serious buyer with a definite buying objective.

Negotiate

Automobile dealers are tough negotiators, for that is their everyday business. Their objective is to get as much money from the deal as possible. Your objective is simple and clear cut: to get the best deal in town. The ability to present a check for that amount, on the spot, can definitely be effective. The amount has to be fair versus a ridiculous unrealistic figure which can result in embarrassment. REMEMBER: If the deal isn't right, walk! Check one or two other dealerships, for negotiating involves people, personalities, and a willingness to bend if necessary. Shopping around makes sense!

Watch out for hooks

The hooks often represent those last minute extras that were not previously discussed. They are the extra services that are nice to have and usually have a high profit margin for the dealer. Some typical examples are as follows:

• Dealer preparation charges, before delivery
• Undercoating
• Exterior paint sealer/wax
• Interior fabric sealer
• Extended warranty

All are worthwhile items, but should be part of the deal at the time of negotiation.

The facts about automobile leasing

Leasing an automobile definitely has advantages as well as disadvantages. **The advantages most often listed are as follows:**

1. The money that would normally be invested in an automobile would be free to be invested in something else that may yield a higher rate of return on investment, (something that appreciates versus something that depreciates).

2. If you own a business and/or use the automobile for business purposes, you may expense (charge off) that portion of the lease payment to the business as a business expense, thus, the tax advantage. Accurate record keeping is required, with actual business use mileage recorded and compared to the total annual miles, in order to determine the final percentage of business use of the lease payment that can be expensed.

3. The lease plan can provide a new automobile on a regular basis, creating fewer maintenance costs. Most of all, the hassle and negotiating process of buying and trading is eliminated.

4. For the average automobile buyer, the cost may represent a monthly payment considerably less than an actual purchase payment, particularly when the buyer might only have the initial minimum required down payment.

5. Finally, for no other reason than a lot of people are doing it, so it must be a good idea for the people that follow trends.

The disadvantages are not often discussed and can be stated simply:

1. Leasing typically costs more in the end versus buying. There will never be any equity (ownership) accumulation, and therefore, it can never be shown on a financial statement, business or personal.

2. Thoroughly compare the figures of the monthly payments. Buying may represent a slightly higher payment, but at the conclusion, you will have a paid for car that will have some worth versus nothing for the leased automobile.

NOTE: Automobile leasing is rapidly gaining in popularity. Recent surveys have shown that almost 25 percent of all new automobiles are leased, and approximately 50 percent of all high priced luxury automobiles are leased. *PEOPLE ARE FOLLOWING TRENDS.*

Shop for deals and read the fine print

The importance of understanding automobile leasing cannot be overstated. The typical contracts are not complicated, but do set forth specific restrictions such as annual mileage allowed within the framework of the lease payment. This is typically 15,000 miles per year. An additional mileage charge of 10 to 15 cents per mile can be added at the conclusion of the lease agreement. Two and three year leases are usually the most popular.

Lease plans will vary, so comparison shopping is necessary in order to obtain the best priced lease program. Programs will vary from dealer to dealer and from deal to deal.

Also, the leasee should compare the advertised leasing rates to the "actual cost" of leasing. An automobile advertised for $289 per month could have an additional suggested capitalized cost reduction charge of $2,500, which represents a nonrefundable payment that covers part of the automobile's depreciation during the term of the lease. This charge could be in the form of an up-front payment or a payment at the end of the lease. The charge can vary between dealers and deals.

If a capitalized cost reduction charge is required, add that to the cost of the lease in order to determine the "actual cost" of leasing. Ford Leasing Publications Center offers some excellent brochures that will answer most leasing questions. The brochures are available upon request by calling (800) 421-0494.

Tips for buying auto insurance

1. Compare Prices

Prices for auto insurance can vary a great deal. Therefore, shopping for price quotations should definitely result in saving dollars. A minimum of 3 or 4 quotes should show a clear picture.

To compare rates, get a quote from your local independent insurance agent, a quote from one or more of the big companies with their home town agents, and one or two quotes from a "direct writer," such as GEICO (800) 841-3000 or Worldwide (800) 325-1487.

2. Check Service

Call a few local auto body repair shops and inquire as to the best companies when it comes to no-hassle-prompt settling of claims. Then compare the list to the price quotations.

3. Ask for Discounts

Discounts for: nonsmokers, nondrinkers, teenagers with good grades, driver education program completion, cars driven less than 7,500 miles per year, air bags, antilock brakes, etc.

Note: The discounts can be confusing. Compare the final costs from each company submitting a quotation. Often the companies that offer the most discounts are at a higher price to start.

Don't Have the Cash?
Put It on the Credit Card!

Quality products being offered at a very competitive price for a limited time stimulates purchasing activity. If it is a product that you need or would like, you will inevitably be thinking seriously about making the purchase.

The current state of the economy has created an extremely competitive retail market, resulting in a lot of "good buys" for consumers. But the issue remains as to what really constitutes a "good buy" once the cost of credit has been calculated into the purchase price.

Here is how it works. Say for example the item that grabs your attention is a quality name brand television set that regularly sells for $895. The GREAT SALE is offering the set at $699 for a limited time only. You have decided that this is definitely a TV that you would like to have for all the right reasons, including the fact this is the lowest price ever. Therefore, you want to act upon it. But you don't have the cash or the necessary balance in your checkbook to comfortably write a check. Bingo, the credit card! The justification is that you are taking advantage of the GREAT SALE, for the TV is nearly $200 off the regular price. The great price at the great sale will only be a great price if you can pay the $699 within 30 days of the first billing cycle of your credit card (thus paying no interest). If you pay the minimum and continue to only pay the minimum amounts, the accrued interest will result in your actually paying much more. Depending on how long you stretch out the payments, you might even end up spending more than the actual price of the TV before the sale. The example on the following page reflects the actual interest paid when making a fixed $25 per month payment for 40 months.

The interest expense could definitely be justified if we were experiencing an inflationary economy for retail consumer goods. But that is definitely not the case in the '90s. For many purchases during the '80s, it made perfect sense to quickly take advantage of sale merchandise and pay later with interest as part of the cost. In the '80s, even with the cost of interest it was still cheaper than waiting and paying the inflationary price. Not so in the '90s! The wisdom of the time suggests patience in waiting for prices to cool even more, to pay with cash and avoid the interest expense (which is no longer an expense that can be claimed on income tax returns).

See example on following page.

CREDIT CARD Purchase with Annual Percentage Rate of Interest 18%
1.5 % per month on the unpaid balance

Purchase: $699.00   Minimum Monthly Payment: $25.00

Month		Month		Month	
Balance 1	699.00	**15**	520.94	**28**	276.26
Interest	10.49		7.81		4.14
Balance 2	684.49	**16**	503.75	**29**	255.41
Interest	10.27		7.56		3.83
Balance 3	669.75	**17**	486.31	**30**	234.24
Interest	10.05		7.29		3.51
Balance 4	654.80	**18**	468.60	**31**	212.75
Interest	9.82		7.03		3.19
5	Skip Payment Christmas Season Offer				
Balance 6	664.62	**19**	450.63	**32**	190.94
Interest	9.97		6.76		2.86
Balance 7	649.59	**20**	432.39	**33**	168.81
Interest	9.74		6.49		2.53
Balance 8	634.33	**21**	413.88	**34**	146.34
Interest	9.52		6.21		2.20
Balance 9	618.85	**22**	395.08	**35**	123.54
Interest	9.28		5.93		1.85
Balance 10	603.13	**23**	376.01	**36**	100.39
Interest	9.05		5.64		1.51
Balance 11	587.18	**24**	356.65	**37**	76.89
Interest	8.81		5.35		1.15
Balance 12	570.99	**25**	337.00	**38**	53.05
Interest	8.56		5.06		0.80
Balance 13	554.55	**26**	317.06	**39**	28.84
Interest	8.32		4.76		0.43
Balance 14	537.87	**27**	296.81	**40**	4.28
Interest	8.07		4.45		0.06

Total Interest PAID: $230.09

PURCHASE + INTEREST = TOTAL (TRUE) COST
$699.00   + $230.09   = $929.09

Note: The above schedule was based upon a firm $25.00 per month payment (the fifth month was skipped as a part of a Christmas Season Offer that is common with many cards). If the payments were accelerated to $75 or $100 per month, the interest charge would be greatly reduced. Typically, the monthly minimum payment due is reduced as the balance is reduced so to extend the payment period (this results in a greater amount of interest earned for the lender/credit card bank).

Recognize credit card costs to merchants and ask for the discount!

Merchants are charged a fee for every credit card transaction processed. The fee for some cards can be fixed, such as a flat 5 percent of the total for every ticket processed. Others will have a sliding scale based upon the dollar amount of an individual transaction or the average dollar amount for the merchant's total number of transactions. For example, if the average transaction was over $700, the fee could be as low as 1.65%. Visa and MasterCard are favored by many merchants because their rates are the most competitive.

Knowing this can help when offering to pay cash. Say for example that you are buying a small cassette tape recorder that sells for $59.95. The batteries are an additional $3.50. At that point you could comfortably say to the merchant, "I will be paying cash today instead of using my credit card, would you be willing to throw in the batteries?" Another example would be if you bought a name brand men's suit of clothing, that regularly sold for $450, at half price for $225. But, because of the half price sale there was a charge for alterations. Same scenario: if the alterations came to $9.75, ask the merchant if that charge could be picked-up by the store in lieu of your immediate cash payment versus using your credit card. You will be amazed as to the number of merchants that will be very pleased to honor your request.

90 days same as cash (a.k.a. no payments until next year!)

Tempting advertising lures offer products now without the immediate concern for payment.

You can purchase a complete living room set with no money down, just your good credit, and no payments for whatever time (90 days, one full year). You may have the choice of paying off the full price at the close of the time period allotted (90 days, etc.), or the contract immediately rolls over into installment payments at the typical 18% annual percentage rate of interest; 1.5% per month on the unpaid balance for the term of the contract; one, two, three or more years.

Your intentions may be to pay off the balance at the assigned date, but unforeseen circumstances may dictate otherwise, leaving you with the payment schedule.

Remember, add the total interest expense with the actual purchase price to determine the total price that you will pay with the use of credit. Then ask yourself how much you could have saved if you had paid cash.

Large chain stores that offer these credit lures may not always be in a position to negotiate for cash, for most chains have strict guidelines for the store manager as well as for commissioned sales people. But if you comparative shop, you will find someone that will negotiate for cash.

When credit becomes too much to handle

The phrases "she went off the deep end" and "man overboard" are definite messages of alarm, concern, worry, and in some cases panic. When used with reference to credit, they can mean being off the deep end financially or thrown into deep, deep debt. The only escape, often times, is bankruptcy. The alarm, concern, worry and panic are even worse if the one in debt is out of work, loses a job or is the victim of an employer cutback.

Too much credit in the '80s

Banks, department stores and finance companies were literally throwing easy credit at consumers during the 1980s. Almost every other month I received preapproved credit applications from Visa, MasterCard, and department stores, as well as instant cash from finance companies offering an unsecured line of credit. My wife was also receiving pre-approved credit, which was very baffling, since she was a homemaker at the time and had been unemployed for over 15 years. The credit world was functioning with a unique set of rules and logic tailored for the '80s.

The fact that becomes very distinct is that the plastic cards may look alike and even have the same name, as is the case with Visa and MasterCard, but in reality they are not the same. Each bank that offers the cards has its own rates, annual fees and transaction fees. Some will offer a pay period of 30 days with no interest, while others start charging interest immediately at the time of purchase if the card had a previous month's balance.

Bankcards with low rates or no fees
Where to find them?

Call **Bankcard Holders of America**
(800) 553-8025

List sells for $4.00 or send a $4.00 check to:

Bankcard Holders of America
560 Herndon Parkway, Suite 120
Herndon, Virginia 22070

Request "The Fair Deal Kit"

Learn and understand what using credit cards actually costs!

The real test for having too much credit is when an individual is only paying the minimum due on the charge account bills. Quite simply, the incoming cash flow (weekly paycheck) cannot handle the amount of credit, for it does not fit into the budget. This happens when a budget is not initially set forth, but later evolves as a consequence of bill paying. Panic sets in when emergencies occur with no money set aside for that "rainy day."

Bite the bullet and take the cure

If credit buying has you locked tight every month, immediately stop credit buying and convert to cash. Then assess how long it will take to pay off the current outstanding bills and commit to a payoff program.

The chart on the following page analyzes what $300.00 per month in savings looks like in five years!

STATEMENT SAVINGS ACCOUNT INTEREST AT 5.88% (5 YEAR AVERAGE)
Monthly Interest: .0049 per month (5.88/12)

Period	deposit	subtotal	interest	balance
1	300.00	-.-	1.47	301.47
2	300.00	601.47	2.95	604.42
3	300.00	904.42	4.43	908.85
4	300.00	1208.85	5.92	1214.77
5	300.00	1514.77	7.42	1522.19
6	300.00	1822.19	8.93	1831.12
13	300.00	4016.75	19.68	4036.43
14	300.00	4336.43	21.25	4357.68
15	300.00	4657.68	22.82	4680.50
16	300.00	4980.50	24.40	5004.90
17	300.00	5304.90	25.99	5330.90
18	300.00	5630.90	27.59	5658.49
25	300.00	7958.02	38.99	7997.02
26	300.00	8297.02	40.66	8337.67
27	300.00	8637.67	42.32	8680.00
28	300.00	8980.00	44.00	9024.00
29	300.00	9324.00	45.69	9369.69
30	300.00	9669.69	47.38	9717.07
37	300.00	12137.40	59.47	12196.87
38	300.00	12496.87	61.23	12558.10
39	300.00	12858.10	63.00	12921.11
40	300.00	13221.11	64.78	13285.89
41	300.00	13585.89	66.57	13652.46
42	300.00	13952.46	68.37	14020.83
49	300.00	16569.25	81.19	16650.44
50	300.00	16950.44	83.06	17033.49
51	300.00	17333.49	84.93	17418.43
52	300.00	17718.43	86.82	17805.25
53	300.00	18105.25	88.72	18193.96
54	300.00	18493.96	90.62	18584.59

	7	8	9	10	11	12
deposit	300.00	300.00	300.00	300.00	300.00	300.00
	2131.12	2441.57	2753.53	3067.02	3382.05	3698.62
interest	10.44	11.96	13.49	15.03	16.57	18.12
	2141.57	2453.53	2767.02	3082.05	3398.62	3716.75

Annual Interest Earned: 116.74

	19	20	21	22	23	24
deposit	300.00	300.00	300.00	300.00	300.00	300.00
	5958.49	6287.69	6618.49	6950.93	7284.98	7620.68
interest	29.20	30.81	32.43	34.06	35.70	37.34
	5987.69	6318.49	6650.93	6984.98	7320.68	7658.02

Annual Interest Earned: 341.28

	31	32	33	34	35	36
deposit	300.00	300.00	300.00	300.00	300.00	300.00
	10017.07	10366.15	10716.95	11069.46	11423.70	11779.68
interest	49.08	50.79	52.51	54.24	55.98	57.72
	10066.15	10416.95	10769.46	11123.70	11479.68	11837.40

Annual Interest Earned: 579.37

	43	44	45	46	47	48
deposit	300.00	300.00	300.00	300.00	300.00	300.00
	14320.83	14691.00	15062.99	15436.80	15812.44	16189.92
interest	70.17	71.99	73.81	75.64	77.48	79.33
	14391.00	14762.99	15136.80	15512.44	15889.92	16269.25

Annual Interest Earned: 831.85

	55	56	57	58	59	60
deposit	300.00	300.00	300.00	300.00	300.00	300.00
	18884.59	19277.12	19671.58	20067.97	20466.30	20866.59
interest	92.53	94.46	96.39	98.33	100.28	102.25
	18977.12	19371.58	19767.97	20166.30	20566.59	20968.83

Annual Interest Earned: $1,099.59

Total Interest Earned $2,968.83

NOTE: The interest rate for statement saving accounts will fluctuate. There will be periods of both low and high rates.

CHAPTER SEVEN

Professional Buying Skills

The top ten things to do all the time

I.	Pay with cash
II.	Use credit cards intelligently
III.	Forward buy where applicable
IV.	Negotiate when possible
V.	Request a price quotation when needed
VI.	Use order sheets when possible
VII.	Barter, if possible
VIII.	Use buying services
IX.	Promote partnerships
X.	Be certain to have it all in writing

I. Pay with cash

Whenever possible, PAY WITH CASH for the following reasons:

1. Cash puts you (the buyer) in a better bargaining position when asking for a cheaper price. You have the psychological advantage.

2. Cash helps you to stay within the boundary of your personal or household budget. This is particularly important for people who have difficulty budgeting or saving; and especially for those people who have the weakness of spending more than they actually earn as income. When businesses have that problem, it is referred to as a "negative cash flow." Our government has that problem annually. Quite simply, more money is going out than is actually coming in.

   If you have or think that you have this negative cash flow problem, immediately convert everything to cash buying. WHY? Obviously, CASH CONTROLS IMPULSE BUYING. If you don't have the cash to buy it, then you won't. Leave the credit cards at home.

3. Cash avoids the interest charges that are associated with extended charge accounts, which are no longer a tax deductible expense.

II. Use credit cards intelligently

When credit cards are used on a short term (30 day) basis, interest charges are usually avoided. Quite simply, the buyer is able to use the credit at no expense. The following benefits are derived when using credit cards:

1. A record of purchases through a detailed monthly statement.
2. A way to track personal or household expenses.
3. A documented record of legitimate tax deductions.
4. Convenience when returning merchandise or obtaining refunds.
   a. simplifies paper work needed
   b. saves time for you and the store

III. Forward buy where applicable

Forward buying is the practice of buying things in a quantity that is greater than currently needed, but yet not beyond foreseeable needs. This can represent an area for triple savings.

A good example of forward buying is in food prices. Prices increase regularly for many non-seasonal items. Therefore, what we pay today will probably be less than what the price will be within the next several months. So, the savings is in buying a given quantity at today's prices. The double savings comes from sale or off-season items that are below today's prices. For instance, most people buy roasts in the winter and steaks in the summer for barbecuing. Therefore, roasts during the winter months and steaks during the summer months will be priced higher. So, if you have a freezer you may save money by buying roasts in the summer and steaks in the winter. Another example is the after Christmas sales; Christmas cards at 50% off, etc., etc.

The forward buyer would buy a quantity to meet a 3, 6, 9 or 12 month usage, a quantity that could conveniently be stored, kept fresh, and would normally be purchased and consumed during that given time period. The triple savings would be in time and gasoline (personal stress where applicable) saved by not having to make as many buying trips to the store.

IV. Negotiate when possible

Negotiation is where the buyer and seller discuss the price with an offer and a counter offer, resulting in an agreed amount. It is fair to say that just about any purchase will represent a potential for negotiation.

The extent of being able to negotiate prices will greatly depend upon the business and economic conditions of each community. If the economy is prospering and businesses are easily selling their goods and services, then the chances for negotiating are somewhat limited. But that is not the common situation in most communities in the '90s. Therefore, now is definitely the time to sharpen your negotiating skills so that you can buy at the lowest possible prices.

The seven steps to professionally negotiating price:

(See chapter three for a complete list of negotiating tips.)

Step 1   Knowledge is power

Begin by answering the following three questions:

1. Do I have a good understanding and knowledge of the product or service that I intend to buy?
2. Do I know the seller's reputation in the community?
3. Do I know the market condition and the extent of competition?

If you can answer "yes" to these questions, then you will be in a favorable negotiating position. If not, then prepare to do the research so that you can comfortably answer these questions. **WHEN NEGOTIATING, KNOWLEDGE IS POWER.**

Example: If you wanted to have the exterior of your house professionally painted, you would do the following:

a. Take a few quick measurements to estimate the total amount of square footage that would be painted.

b. Call a reputable paint store and ask the yield per gallon, that is how much per gallon is needed to paint the type of surface (siding) that you have. The person at the paint store will typically tell you that 300-400 square feet per gallon is normal, depending upon the surface, and if applied by brush or spray. At that point, you can calculate the rest, and while not being totally accurate, can come fairly close to the actual amount of paint needed to do the job. Price per gallon multiplied by number of gallons will reveal a reasonably good estimate as to the total cost of the paint.

c. Another call to the paint store can obtain the names of a few reputable professional painters, along with the going wage per hour that a good painter receives.

d. Call two or three painters and request each to bid on doing your painting job. With each bid identify the specific paint that will be used (if you have a brand preference, then request it be used), the quantity needed (how many gallons), and the estimated amount of time necessary to complete the work. After you have that information, along with checking work references, then you can intelligently make the buying/hiring decision.

NOTE: If the bids are all too high, then perhaps you need a few more bids, or the painters may all be busy and you may want to consider waiting a few months.

e. Once you have selected the person to do the work, you just might want to pop the question, "Would you give a discount for cash? Not a check, but cash?" If you pay by cash, when the work is completed to your satisfaction, then the painter can give you a signed receipt for receiving payment in full which will be adequate for your records. Remember, you have nothing to lose by asking.

Step 2   Develop a price awareness

Find out what the competitive prices are for the same or similar products or services. The larger the amount of the purchase, the greater the importance of having a thorough and complete pricing knowledge. Also, the greater the dollar amount involved, the greater the potential to negotiate.

Example: If you purchased a new home and needed to do the complete landscaping you would do the following:

a. Seek the professional assistance of someone that could help you with a landscape layout and design, along with identifying the type of plants and shrubs that you like and that would grow on your site.

b. Assuming that you plan on doing the planting yourself, you would then call several nurseries for price quotations.

c. Based upon the number of plants and shrubs and the dollar amount that you would be spending, you would then be in a position to determine if you could negotiate price. Again, the greater the dollar amount involved, the greater the potential to negotiate.

Step 3   Establish price objectives

Establish the minimum price that you would expect to pay and the maximum price that you would pay. The final price that is actually paid will probably be somewhere between your low and high figures. Be careful not to reveal these figures to the seller when negotiating.

Example: If the asking price of a house that you were very serious about buying was $112,000, you would have to first determine your price objectives; the minimum price you would offer, and the maximum price you would be willing to pay.

Then, after inquiring how long the house has been on the market and how anxious the seller is to negotiate price, you would then submit your first offer, say $100,000. You could possibly buy it for that price, but most likely the response would be a counter offer for $110,000. Then, it could go back and forth once or twice and you could settle on perhaps $106,000. Your initial price objectives may have been a minimum of $100,000 and a maximum of $108,000. If that was the case then you would be in good shape at $106,000.

Note: When buying real estate it is important to be able to identify the following:

a. The economic conditions that exist within your community, a seller's or a buyer's market.

b. The reputation of the seller (real estate listing office, if being sold through a realtor) in setting prices. Do the prices represent fair market value or above market prices?

c. Prices of comparable homes that have recently sold within the last 30 to 60 days.

d. The type of neighborhood, trendy and popular, average, not popular, young families or retired, etc.

e. The length of time that the property has been on the market. If over a year, why?

Step 4   Find out who can actually do the negotiating

Before negotiating can even be considered, it is essential that you are dealing with the right person; the person in the organization who can actually do the negotiating. Do not be shy in asking to talk with the manager or owner. Then, do not be embarrassed to ask the question: "Will you negotiate the price for cash or favorable terms?" The worst that can happen is to be told "no." If that does occur, you can confidently admit that you are shopping for the best value, and then leave. If it's merchandise that you think can be negotiated, then you will eventually find someone who will be pleased to be able to negotiate with you.

There are certain situations when negotiating will not be applicable, such as a large department store. As a rule, the managers must follow the company pricing policy. But to satisfy your curiosity, you still could ask.

Step 5   Negotiate in private

Negotiating should be conducted in a comfortable situation. An audience will tend to make the negotiating process a bit awkward. So, when inquiring, do it in a quiet corner of the store or in the manager's office. **BE PROFESSIONAL!**

Step 6   Use cash "psychologically"

This situation is when the old saying, "money talks," can often be successfully applied. The sight and smell of money actually presented to the seller can help to successfully conclude the negotiating process. This cash will represent the buyer's final effort of strength. If it does not succeed, the buyer will have to change price objectives or search for another seller.

Example: Cash could easily be used when submitting an offer to buy that next set of tires for your car. Say that you are quoted $325 for a set of quality replacement tires and a front end alignment. You put $300 in cash on the counter and ask if that will be acceptable, for that is all that you are able to spend. No check, no credit card, CASH. That's a reasonable offer and represents less than a 10 percent discount with no risk to the seller. A lot of factors may be involved, but odds are in your favor.

Step 7   Keep a poker face and be professional

The way to accomplish this professionalism is by practice. Practice by make-believe role playing situations with friends or relatives. You play the role of the buyer and let someone else be the seller. Then, play the game by both being tough. Don't laugh, this is how the professionals as well as many governments train their negotiators. By the time you are ready to negotiate with a real seller, you will have anticipated most of the questions and alternatives that could arise. This will allow you to feel very confident about your negotiating ability.

The following example will demonstrate the seven step negotiation procedure:

You want to buy a specific make and model stereo system

Step 1

You have a good understanding and knowledge of the make and model stereo system that you intend to buy. You were able to obtain that information from a catalog and brochure, plus by examining the actual system. As for the stereo store's reputation, you know that it will negotiate price and has been in business for over ten years. It occasionally advertises sales on selected merchandise, and many of your friends have recommended the store, having had good experiences with quality and service. Competition in the community is keen among stereo stores. Therefore, the conditions for negotiating are good.

Step 2

You take the time to telephone several stores that sell the make and model stereo system that you intend to buy. You find that prices range from a high of $825 to a low of $795.

Step 3

You determine your price objectives. The maximum price that you would pay is $795, and the minimum price that you would like to pay is $695, which represents a 12.5 percent discount off the $795. Your good judgement and an educated guess arrive at that number as being a fair price for the seller and a good deal for you. That is about all that you have to act upon, for there is no real way of easily finding out the stereo system's actual cost or mark-up.

It is important to remember that in trying to determine a minimum price objective, you must be fair and realistic. There are no set rules or guidelines, just good judgement. The seller must be able to make a profit in order to remain in business, remember that!

Step 4

You call the store and talk to the manager, who informs you that the stereo system that you wanted is available and that your business would be appreciated. A mutually convenient time is arranged to meet and discuss the terms for a possible purchase transaction.

Step 5

You meet the manager and inspect the stereo system. It is exactly what you want to buy. You then privately begin to negotiate the price.

Step 6

You offer to pay the manager $695 cash, realizing that there probably will be some negotiating. The manager counters with $745. Then, you show the actual cash. You settle on $725 as being a fair price. The cash represents an immediate payment, without having to do a personal check bank verification or have the expense of processing a credit card transaction.

Step 7

You have proven yourself to be a professional buyer and conclude the transaction with a hand shake. The manager expresses gratitude for your business and a sincere invitation to return for any other need that you may have in the future. **NEGOTIATING IS JUST THAT SIMPLE!**

V. Request a bid or price quotation

This process would be applicable when purchasing expensive "big ticket" items such as computer equipment. The procedure would be as follows:

1. Determine who and how many will do the bidding. That is, who will you be contacting for bids, and how many bids will you actually need? The answer to this will be left to your good judgement. You may be satisfied with as little as two bids, or to be thorough, you may want as many as six. As a rule, three to five would be adequate. A quick look in the telephone directory yellow pages will provide the names and addresses of the businesses that offer the product or service you wish to buy. If possible, select the businesses that have the reputation for being competitive.

2. Draft a letter that will professionally request the bid or price quotation. The letter should be addressed to the manager or owner of each business and include the following:

   • The name and product specifications. Describe every detail about the product so that there will definitely be no misunderstanding regarding the exact product.
   • The quantity to be purchased.
   • The latest date bids will be accepted.
   • The method in which the bids will be evaluated. Such as, the purchase being awarded to the lowest bidder.
   • The method of payment and delivery.

   Financial arrangements are critical. You may already have the necessary funds as part of your personal cash savings, or you may need to check with a bank or lending institution to arrange for credit. Whatever the situation, remember, it will add to your professionalism as the buyer if you are prepared.

The following is an example of a letter requesting a bid for specified computer equipment.

January 10, 199x

Your Name
Complete Mailing Address
Telephone Number

Mr. John Sample, Manager
Metropolitan Computers
100 Main Street
Hometown, USA 00000

Dear Mr. Sample:

I am offering your store an invitation to submit a competitive bid on the following specified computer equipment:

(The equipment must be described in complete detail)

The bid must be submitted in writing no later than January 25, 199x. The purchase will be awarded on February 1, 199x to the store with the lowest bid.

The payment will be in the form of a cashier's check payable to the store upon delivery at the store.

Submit the bid to:
Your Name
Complete Mailing Address

Respectfully,

Your Name

3. When bidding is requested for a service to be performed, first request a proposal as to how the bidder intends to render the service, or what materials would be used, to assure the buyer exactly what the bid price will represent. An example when this procedure would be used is in building or remodeling a home, for it enables the buyer to compare bids for identical materials and services.

This procedure can also be done when trying to determine the cost of repair work. You may be confronted with the complicated decision: do I have it fixed, do I try to fix it myself, or is it worth fixing at all.

The following example demonstrates the type of information that a bid should provide. Do I have the refrigerator fixed? Do I try to fix it myself (if I have the skill)? Or is it worth fixing at all? Then the decision is yours based upon the facts.

REPAIR WORK EVALUATION

Name of Company _City Appliance Service_
Address _246 Central Avenue_
Big City, USA 99999

Phone _555-5678_   Date _Feb. 10 199x_

Item needing repair _Refrigerator_
Make _Popular_   Model _17C_ Serial No. _K55_
Cause of Breakdown _Electrical, it sparked_

Parts and Materials

Quantity	Description	Unit Cost	Total
1	Compressor	-	307.00
1	Kit	-	32.50
2	Clamps	10.25	20.50
Total Cost of Parts and Materials			360.00

Labor (actual or estimated)

Worker	Started	Finished	Hours	Rate/hr.	Total
Estimated time			3	40.	120.
Total Cost of Labor					120.

TOTAL COST OF REPAIR _480._

4. The bid procedure helps to determine fair competitive prices, but does not always assure the buyer of the lowest possible prices, depending upon who is submitting bids. If all the suppliers in your community are traditionally higher priced, then the bids will be commensurate with their reputations. So, you may want to consider requesting bids from suppliers outside your community, or you may want to try negotiating before requesting bids.

When bids are received, they should be conveniently recorded on a bid sheet. The bid sheet should include the following information:

• The quantity to be purchased.

• A complete item description of the product.

• The names of the suppliers contacted for bids.

• The unit price for each item.

• The total prices for all the items.

The example BID SHEET on the following page demonstrates its actual use. It records three bids on selected furniture items. The lowest bids are circled and then totaled.

NOTE: Furniture items were specifically selected for the example because they represent items that many people do not comparatively shop for, often paying more for a lesser quality.

BID SHEET

DATE _Feb. 14, 199x_

QUANTITY	DESCRIPTION	Supplier House of Furniture UNIT PRICE	TOTAL	Supplier Southside Furniture UNIT PRICE	TOTAL	Supplier Warehouse Direct Furniture UNIT PRICE	TOTAL
1	Lazy Recliner Mod. 7-4		392.50		(369.00)		374.00
2	Granville K-Series Table	119.00	238.00	123.00	246.00	108.00	(216.00)
2	Deuco Lamp. H-136-D	74.95	149.90	62.50	(125.00)	79.00	158.00
	TOTALS				494.00		216.00

VI. Use order sheets when possible

The completed order sheet will represent a specific list of the items to be purchased. The advantages of having such a list are twofold:

1. To reduce the risk of forgetting things, which may result in having to make a second trip to the store.

2. To help control spending if the buyer just purchases the items that are listed on the order sheet, (particularly helpful for the impulse buyer who is trying to stay within a certain budget).

Experience will prove that the time it takes to fill out an order sheet will result in convenience and cost savings.

The example on the following page demonstrates the use of an order sheet for grocery items, which would be among the more popular uses.

NOTE: The example given (grocery buying) can represent one of the largest areas for cash control savings for most families.

ORDER SHEET

CANNED GOODS	FROZEN FOODS
2 Applesauce	3 (12oz) Apple Juice
3 Tomato Soup	4 Chicken Pot Pies
2 Fruit Cocktail	1 lrg Sausage Pizza
1 Sweet Peas	
BREADS/BAKERY	**DAIRY PRODUCTS**
2 White Bread	2 gal Milk
1/2 doz Danish	1/2 lb Swiss Cheese
1 doz Hotdog Buns	1 doz Large Eggs
FRESH FRUITS	**MEATS**
2 lb Pears	5 lbs Ground Beef
1 Pineapple	1 pkg Hotdogs
3 lb Apples	1 lb Bacon
2 lbs. Peaches	
PAPER PRODUCTS	**MISC.**
2 rolls Paper Towels	2 pkg Jello
1 pkg Napkins	1 jar Relish

VII. Barter, if possible

One of the easiest and simplest ways of acquiring things is by trading for them. History provides us with countless examples of how people and nations traded products and services to fulfill their needs. Children are natural traders with baseball cards, marbles, toys, and occasionally some of Mom's sack lunches.

It is not hard to do, IF YOU ARE SERIOUS ABOUT DOING IT.

Bartering begins by assessing the things that you could offer as trade to someone else who may need them. Ideally, if you have a given skill or even several skills, they could be offered in the form of a rendered service. Once you have determined the things that you would be able to trade, appraise them in terms of their value. Say for example, how much is your time worth as a handy-person, fixer-upper, painter, gardener, window washer, evening janitorial person, typist, computer worker, or whatever else.

If your appraisal is realistic and fair, and your work is good, you have something to trade. Do not be shy in asking the question, "Would you be willing to trade for my services?"

NOTE: THIS WORKS AND CAN REPRESENT AN AREA FOR TREMENDOUS CASH SAVINGS.

VIII. Use buying services

Many communities have businesses that specialize in offering reduced prices to their customers. These businesses may be referred to as membership discount stores, co-operatives, brokerages, etc. They may be open to the public at no cost, or they may require an initial membership fee. Whatever the case may be, they usually represent an opportunity to save substantially, and therefore, should always be considered when comparing prices. Check your telephone directory for listings.

An example of information buying services are those organizations that provide automobile financial facts that make a critical difference when buying a new or used car. *The information provided is as follows:*

- new car prices
  (wholesale and retail)
- used car valuations
  (high and low)
- option prices
- computer print outs comparing retail and dealer invoices, specifications, safety features, and repair records.

Some of the services for automobile buying facts are as follows:

- AAA Auto Pricing Service (900) 776-4222
- Car/Puter's Instant Pricing Hotline (900) 370-AUTO
- Nationwide Auto Brokers (800) 521-7257
- Car Bargains (800) 475-7283 (information and bidding service)
- Edmund's Car Price Buyers Guide available at bookstores (domestic cars, foreign cars and truck editions).

IX. Promote Partnerships

Occasions arise when sharing some of the work and responsibilities of a service to be performed can be profitable. The prime situations when partnerships can be promoted are when you personally can be involved as a working partner in doing some of the work. Begin by assessing your present skills and abilities, and the potential for acquiring new ones. Then, simply ask the seller, "Can I save some money by being a partner to the work?" If conditions are competitive and the seller wants the business bad enough, an equitable agreement usually can be reached.

Example:

Assume that your single story home needed a new roof. You thought about doing the work yourself, but were concerned that you would not be able to do the job correctly. So, you considered hiring a professional roofing contractor that would guarantee the work, but thought that you probably would not be able to afford the cost.

The following steps should then be taken:

• Determine the total cost if you did everything yourself.

• Ask the professional roofing contractor for a job proposal which includes a cost breakdown of materials and labor.

• Propose the partnership. That is, ask the roofing contractor if you could do some of the work yourself. Specify what you would like to do, such as, stripping off the old roof, and replacing any damaged wood. Then, ask for a revised cost with you as the working partner.

The possible benefiting result of such a partnership would be:

a. The work would be professionally completed accompanied with a workmanship guarantee

b. The final cost may be the same or less than doing it all yourself. How could it be less, you ask? Because the contractor is able to purchase the roofing materials at a far less cost than what you would have to pay. The cost difference involved may be large enough to cover his labor installation charge and still be cheaper than what you would actually pay for the materials alone.

c. The contractor (seller) would be able to make the sale by being competitive.

Work partnerships can be very beneficial for you and the seller.

X. Be certain to have it all in writing

Often, when terms and conditions are discussed, they may assume a different meaning to different people. Therefore, the terms and conditions associated with the purchase of a product or service should be clearly detailed in writing as a contract. It is always advisable to play safe by taking the time to do it right, when in doubt, or as a matter of personal policy; for it is not being out of place to ask the seller to provide you with a detailed and understandable contract. This will simply add to your professionalism as a buyer. If the seller refuses or is reluctant, then you may want to consider doing business with someone else.

Checklist to remember

Who to buy from ...

1. Look for credibility
2. Look for authority
3. Avoid buying as a result of pressure or from a sense of obligation
4. Establish good relationships with people whom you regularly do business
5. If you have been dealt with unfairly, then tell them about it

What to buy ...

1. Analyze value
2. Determine specifications or features

When to buy ...

1. Never buy anything in haste
2. Know how the stores in your community price and merchandise
3. If possible, wait for prices to cool off

Where to buy ...

1. Evaluate the places where you are currently buying
2. Recognize the signs of a good place to buy
3. Consider the buying expense

Why buy ...

1. Define your buying objective
2. Consider doing it yourself
3. Consider renting

How to buy ...

1. Pay with cash
2. Use credit cards intelligently
3. Forward buy where applicable
4. Negotiate when possible
5. Request a bid or price quotation when needed
6. Use order sheets when possible
7. Barter if possible
8. Use buying services
9. Promote partnerships
10. Be certain, have it all in writing

Conclusion

Economic security during the '90s cannot be taken for granted. The current state of the economy has definitely "knocked some sense" into people who are overspending and are caught-up in buying binges. As a result, many are struggling with debt.

Retailers are stressed because overall spending is down due to the current conservative attitude of consumers who are worried and concerned about the climate of economic uncertainty.

If you can reduce your debt and strengthen your cash position, you will come out financially stronger and with acquired cash buying skills that can benefit you for the rest of your life.

THE **POWER** OF **CASH** DEALS

Appendix

The forms contained in this Appendix
may be photocopied for actual use.

(forms)

Repair Work Evalution
Bid Sheet
Order Sheet

REPAIR WORK EVALUATION

Name of Company _____

Address _____

_____

Phone _____ Date _____

Item needing repair _____

Make _____ Model _____ Serial No. _____

Cause of Breakdown _____

Parts and Materials

Quantity	Description	Unit Cost	Total

Total Cost of Parts and Materials

Labor (actual or estimated)

Worker	Started	Finished	Hours	Rate/hr.	Total

Total Cost of Labor

TOTAL COST OF REPAIR _____

BID SHEET

DATE _____

Quantity	Description	Supplier		Supplier		Supplier	
		Unit Price	Total	Unit Price	Total	Unit Price	Total
	Totals						

ORDER SHEET

THE **POWER** OF **CASH** DEALS

Index

Additional References

CITIBANK MASTERCARD AND VISA HAS PUBLISHED A SERIES OF BOOKLETS ON PERSONAL FINANCE AS PART OF ITS "KEEPING YOUR FINANCIAL BALANCE" SEMINARS PROGRAM THAT IS BEING CONDUCTED FOR CONSUMERS AROUND THE COUNTRY.

These booklets include:

"Money Matters for Women"
"Money Matters for College Students"
"Money Matters for Young Adults"
"Coping With a Credit Crisis"

One copy of each of these booklets is available free of charge to individuals wanting help with managing their finances.

CITIBANK MONEY MATTERS HOTLINE:
(800) 669-2635